SIERRA VIEW CHILDREN'S

827-0169

The Spanish
Exploration of
the Southwest

 EXPLORATION AND DISCOVERY

EXPLORATION
AND DISCOVERY

The Spanish Exploration of the Southwest

The 16th-century journeys of Cabeza de Vaca
and Coronado through the desert lands
of the American Southwest

Lenore Wilson

Mason Crest Publishers
Philadelphia

Mason Crest Publishers
370 Reed Road
Broomall PA 19008

Mason Crest Publishers' world wide web address is
www.masoncrest.com

First printing

1 3 5 7 9 8 6 4 2

Library of Congress Cataloging-in-Publication Data
on file at the Library of Congress

ISBN 1-59084-055-0

EXPLORATION AND DISCOVERY

Contents

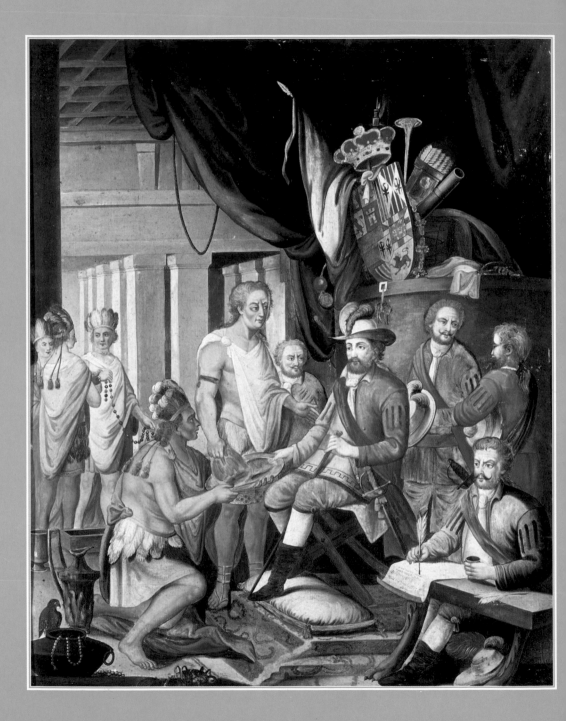

The Spanish Empire Grows

THE YEAR 1492 marked two great milestones for King Ferdinand and Queen Isabella, the rulers of Spain. Nearly eight centuries of warfare between Christians and the Moors, a Muslim tribe from North Africa that had invaded the Iberian peninsula several hundred years earlier, had ended in victory for the Christian king and queen that year. In addition, a sailor named Christopher Columbus had come upon a whole new world. The Spanish felt two such extraordinary events in a single year were proof that God was on their side. In 1493, Pope Alexander VI, himself a Spaniard, lent that belief his official approval. Citing the "authority of the mighty God," the pope solemnly awarded

Christopher Columbus's voyage west across the Atlantic in the fall of 1492 would prove to be a milestone in world history. Columbus returned to Spain convinced that he had found the Far East. This would mean that Spain could set up a fast trade route with China, Japan, and other countries of Asia. It soon became apparent, however, that Columbus had instead found large landmasses that had been unknown to Europeans of his time—the Americas.

Francisco Pizarro was a shrewd and ruthless military leader. He gained fame and wealth by conquering the Incas, the most powerful native civilization of South America, during the 1530s.

to his homeland the right to claim the entire New World so that all of its peoples could be brought to Christ—by kindness and praise if possible, by force of arms if necessary. The same religious enthusiasm that had finally driven the Moors from Spain would now be let loose upon a whole field of new nonbelievers.

To persuade Spanish soldiers to take part in the holy war against the Moors, the rulers of Spain had offered them a big share in the *spoils* of war. Now, the Spanish king made the same offer to get adventurers to try their luck across the Atlantic. As the lands controlled by Spain grew, so would the fortunes of its soldiers.

Hernán Cortés

Hernán Cortés was born in Estremadura, a province of Spain. He traveled to Santo Domingo in the West Indies in 1504, and took part in the conquest of Cuba in 1511. The governor of Cuba was interested in the mainland to the west of the island and picked Cortés to direct the expedition.

Cortés, along with 650 men, explored the Yucatán coast, landing on the coast of Mexico in 1519. There, Cortés founded the settlement of Veracruz. He left soldiers to guard Veracruz, then led the main force overland to Tenochtitlán, the capital of the Aztec empire. Cortés was greeted by Montezuma, the Aztec ruler. The Spaniard soon made Montezuma a prisoner and used him to govern the country.

The Aztecs didn't like Cortés ordering their leader around, so they attacked the soldiers in Tenochtitlán. After a major defeat that came to be known as *La Noche Triste* (the Sorrowful Night), Cortés conquered the Aztec armies on the plain of Otumba. He returned to Tenochtitlán, which he destroyed. On its ruins he built the city that would become the capital of the land, which he renamed New Spain.

Cortés spent the next years spreading Spanish rule. In 1536, he directed an expedition that founded the first settlement in Lower California.

Eventually, Cortés fell out of favor with the king. He died at a small village near Seville, Spain, in 1547. His body was taken back to Mexico to be buried.

The **conquistadors** seized such places as Puerto Rico, Jamaica, and Cuba. Hernán Cortés conquered the Aztecs, taking Mexico with its riches. Francisco Pizarro crushed the Incas of Peru and took their treasures. The Spanish also laid claim to Central America, most of South America, and the islands of the Caribbean. They were more than eager to expand their domain north of the area of Mexico that Cortés had conquered and renamed New Spain. "We came here to serve God and his majesty," one conquistador said, "to give light to those who were in the darkness and to get rich, as all men desire to do." Alvar Núñez Cabeza de Vaca was one of those men.

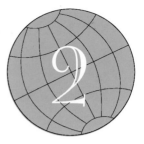

Rough Seas Abroad

THE JOURNEY of Alvar Núñez Cabeza de Vaca remains one of the most amazing feats of exploration in the Americas. By wits, stamina, and luck, four people out of a land force of 300 men found their way back to civilization after eight harrowing years and traversing almost 6,000 miles of mostly unknown territories of North America. They were the first Europeans to report back on the lands that today are the states of Florida, Texas, New Mexico, and Arizona, as well as the northwestern region of Mexico.

Cabeza de Vaca was born in the Spanish province of Jerez de la Frontera around 1480. Little is known about his early life, except that he decided to make his career in the

The name Cabeza de Vaca—which means Head of Cow—began as a title of honor from the Battle of Las Navas de Tolosa in the Sierra Morenas on July 12, 1212. During that battle, a Spanish peasant named Alhaja found an unguarded pass. He marked it with a cow's skull and told leaders of the Christian army based in Navarre, a part of what today is Spain. The army from Navarre used the pass to make a surprise attack on a Moorish army. After winning this battle, King Sancho of Navarre gave the title Cabeza de Vaca to the peasant Alhaja in thanks for his service.

military while he was still in his teens. As a young man Cabeza de Vaca fought in many battles for King Ferdinand and Queen Isabella of Spain. He later served in the army of their grandson, King Charles, when he became ruler of Spain in 1516.

In 1526, King Charles appointed Cabeza de Vaca treasurer of an expedition to explore the region called La Florida. This would include the western coast of what today is the state of Florida and the lands to the north and west. The boundary would be the Rio de las Palmas (River of Palms) in the north of Mexico. As treasurer, Cabeza's job would be to make sure that the king received his share of any treasure the explorers found. The leader of the expedition was a tough conquistador named Pánfilo de Narváez.

Pánfilo de Narváez

Pánfilo De Narváez was born in Valladolid, Spain, in 1470. He became a soldier and left Spain to live in the Spanish colony on Hispaniola. There, he hoped to win fame and fortune as a conquistador.

Narváez served in Hispaniola's military garrison for six years, helping to fight the native Taino people of the island. In 1509 he accompanied Juan de Esquirel to Jamaica, an island to the west. After helping Esquirel conquer Jamaica, Narváez was given his own troops to command. He was sent to Cuba in 1511 and ordered to conquer the island. During the next seven years, Narváez set about this task with ruthless efficiency. A Spanish missionary named Bartholomew de las Casas, who wrote about the conquistadors in the New World, said that Narváez's men massacred thousands of Native Americans.

In 1520, Diego Velasquez, the Spanish governor of Cuba, sent Narváez to take over command of an expedition to Mexico, which had landed there a year earlier under Hernán Cortés. However, Cortés was not willing to give up the leadership without a fight. His troops surprised Narváez—he lost an eye in the fighting—and Cortés imprisoned him for two years while he completed his conquest of Mexico.

Narváez returned to Spain and asked the king to let him lead a new expedition. In 1527 he was given permission to explore the unknown region to the northwest of Cuba known as La Florida.

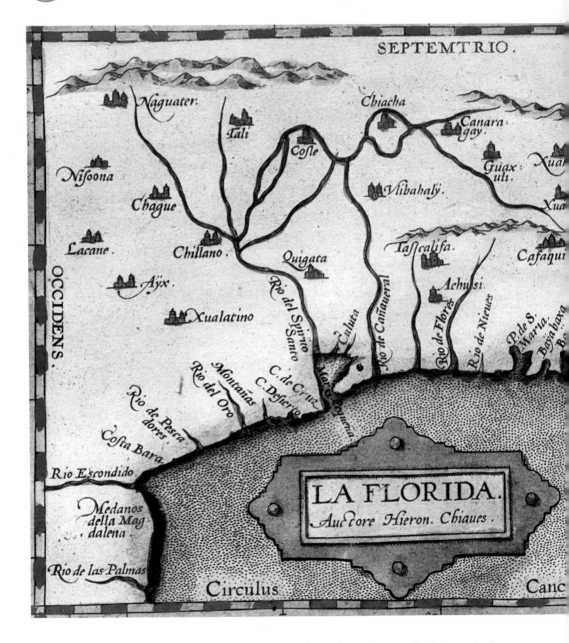

On June 27, 1527, Narváez and Cabeza de Vaca left Spain with six ships and about 500 soldiers.

Their fleet was battered by a hurricane, which sank one of the ships. But weather was not the only problem Narváez

A Spanish map of the land that Juan Ponce de León had named La Florida. Ponce had landed in Florida in 1513 and claimed it for Spain. When he returned in 1521 to establish a settlement in Florida, he was mortally wounded by a poisoned arrow. Pánfilo de Narváez traveled to Florida hoping to succeed where Ponce had failed. The Rio de las Palmas—the western boundary of the Florida region that Narváez had been given permission to explore—can be seen at the lower left side of this map.

and Cabeza de Vaca faced. When they stopped at Hispaniola, about 140 of the men they had brought with them from Spain **deserted** on the island. Over the winter, the two leaders recruited new soldiers and gathered

Native Americans of Florida attack a village in this illustration by the 16th-century artist Theodore de Bry. The Spanish did not have much trouble subduing the Indians on the Caribbean islands where they settled; however, they found the natives living on the mainland to be much fiercer fighters.

provisions for their expedition. By the spring, they were ready to sail for Florida.

In April 1528, Narváez 's five ships carried about 400 men to a bay on the west coast of Florida. This probably was in the area that is now called Tampa Bay.

After landing, however, Narváez made a tactical mistake. He decided to split his forces. He would lead about 300 of the men into the Florida wilderness, while the ships would sail farther along the coast. The plan was for the land and sea expeditions to meet up later. Cabeza de Vaca was against this plan, but Narváez decided to go ahead anyway. He had heard that there was a rich city at a place called Apalachen. This is the site of the present-day city of Tallahassee.

The expedition headed northwest, crossed the Suwannee River, and captured Apalachen. However, the rich city they had hoped to find did not exist. Instead, it was a small native village, and there was no gold. Discouraged, the Spanish army headed southwest to meet with the ships. Along the way, the Spaniards' numbers dwindled because of disease and attacks by hostile Native Americans.

When Narváez reached the coast in August of 1528, he saw no sign of his ships. They had patrolled the waters for a while, but had sailed back to New Spain to get supplies. The surviving members of the expedition were reduced to huddling in a coastal swamp and eating their horses. Narváez ordered the men to build rafts. For the next two weeks, the Spaniards cut down trees, made sails from clothing, wove horsehair into ropes, and melted down metal to make nails. In these crude rafts, they hoped to follow the coast to Spanish settlements in Mexico.

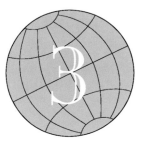

Searching for Fortune

FIVE SMALL BOATS carrying the 250 survivors of the Narváez expedition set out for New Spain, the Spanish colony in Mexico, on September 22, 1528. The men suffered from water shortages, and storms, starvation, native attacks, and disease reduced the expedition's numbers. The rafts followed the shore until the end of October, when a powerful current of fresh water swept them far out into the Gulf of Mexico. They had just found the mouth of the Mississippi River.

Shortly after this, a hurricane hit. The barges carrying Narváez and Cabeza de Vaca were separated. Narváez is believed to have drowned at sea. Cabeza de Vaca and his companions were shipwrecked on an island near Texas on November 6, 1528.

The island—today called Galveston Island—was occupied by Karankawa Indians, who provided them with food. Soon the survivors from another barge joined them. This barge had been commanded by Alonso de Castillo and Andrés Dorantes, who had brought along a black slave named Estéban. This brought the number of Spanish survivors to about 80.

Through the winter, the Spaniards stayed with these natives. In his writings later, Cabeza de Vaca described them as tall and well-built and said he was touched by their goodness. "These people love their offspring more than any in the world and treat them very kindly," he wrote. "If a son dies, the whole village joins the parents and kindred in weeping. The parents set off the wails each day before dawn, again at noon, and at sunset for one year. . . . The people are generous to each other with what little they have."

The winter was very harsh, and the cold, starvation, and fever left just 15 men alive. Cabeza de Vaca and another man, Lope de Oviedo, were very sick. The 13 Spaniards set out in the spring, leaving the two sick men behind with a group of Native Americans, the Churruco, who lived on the mainland.

At first, the Churruco welcomed the newcomers, but, as

Estéban

Also known as **Black Stephen** or **Estevanico**, Estéban was probably the first person of African heritage to travel in the American southwest. He was born around 1503 in the port city of Azemmour in western Morocco. During fighting between Morocco and Portugal, Azemmour was captured by the Portuguese in 1513. Around 1520, the Portuguese sold many Moroccans, including Estéban, into slavery.

Estéban became the servant of Andrés Dorantes, a nobleman from the Castille province of Spain. He was treated well, and the two men became good friends. In 1527, Dorantes joined Pánfilo de Narváez's expedition to Florida.

The expedition was a disaster, and nearly everyone died along the way. Estéban and Dorantes were among the few who survived, arriving in New Spain after wandering through the American southwest for seven years.

Estéban would return to the region. He was sent on a Spanish expedition led by the priest Fray Marcos de Niza, who was searching for the legendary Seven Cites of Cibola. Accounts differ about his fate. Marcos was told that Estéban had been killed by the Zuni Indians. However, some stories indicate that this was a lie so Estéban could escape slavery. If this is true, the Zuni apparently allowed Estéban to live among them and raise a family.

Cabeza de Vaca was to remember, "Half the natives died from a disease of the bowels and blamed us." Once Cabeza de Vaca was well enough to work, he was treated like a slave and made to gather food and carry firewood. During the winter, this tribe ate edible roots that grew under water. In pulling these roots, Cabeza de Vaca's hands became so sore "that a light brush with a piece of straw would cause them to bleed." Blackberries also grew on the mainland, and there were beds of oysters on the shores of these bays. There was little timber near the beach on the mainland, but far-ther inland, the country was forested.

Cabeza de Vaca eventually escaped from this tribe and traveled inland. In order to survive, he learned Indian ways. He walked through the wilderness and traded with tribes that lived many miles from the sea, exchanging colorful seashells for food. The shells were valued by inland Indians, who didn't have tools for cutting mesquite beans. Cabeza de Vaca collected hides and red *ochre*, which was used for dye, flints for arrowheads, and canes for arrow shafts. While walking, he often endured freezing temperatures. He did not go out in the winters, which were so cold that even the Indians remained indoors.

In 1532, near the Colorado River in Texas, Cabeza de Vaca encountered three other members of the Narváez expedition: Castillo, Dorantes, and Estéban. They had been

Red-headed Alvar Núñez Cabeza de Vaca, along with his companions Alonso de Castillo, Andrés Dorantes, and the black slave Estéban, look out over the southwest. The first Europeans to cross the North American continent, their amazing journey took seven years and 6,000 miles.

captured and enslaved by Native Americans, but were ready to try to escape to New Spain.

Dorantes was a slaves of the Mariames, a hunting and gathering group. They enslaved Cabeza de Vaca as well. About this tribe he wrote: "They cast away their daughters at birth; the dogs eat them. They do this because all the nations of the region are their enemies, with whom they war ceaselessly and if they were to marry off their daughters, the daughters would multiply their enemies."

Castillo and Estéban were captives of the Yaguazes. The Yaguazes were known as well-built archers. Their food mainly came from digging roots. They ate deer and fish, too, but often were so hungry they ate "spiders, ant eggs, worms, and lizards, salamanders, snakes, and poisonous vipers." They also ate dirt, rotten wood, and even deer dung. Besides these foods, the Yaguazes ate "other things" that Cabeza de Vaca could not bring himself even to record. He said, "My observations lead me to believe that they would eat stones if there were any in the land."

It took two years before the surviving Spaniards were ready to strike out across the continent. In 1534 they they headed west and south. Their incredible journey lasted two years. Their exact route is unclear, but it seems they traveled across the vast deserts of present-day Texas, perhaps into New Mexico and Arizona, and through Mexico's northern provinces. They followed the Rio Grande north, then then south again into what would become northern Mexico, moving from one tribe to the next. Of the Indians the four men met, Cabeza de Vaca wrote, "they all differ in their habitations, villages, and tongues."

The Spaniards earned reputations as powerful medicine men. They examined sick people and mimicked tribal medicine men by chanting and blowing on afflicted areas. The Indians had no idea the men were chanting Christian prayers they had learned as boys. The Indians gave them gifts because they believed the Spaniards came from heaven.

Estéban was especially honored as a healer. One tribe gave him a rattle made out of a **gourd**. Distant tribes were amazed when he rattled the gourd over men and women to chase illnesses out of them. As the four wandered, he learned complex tribal languages and served as the group's *interpreter*. Tribes also gave the medicine men beans, pumpkins, and blankets made of deer hide.

After many months, Cabeza de Vaca and his party crossed the Rio Grande somewhere near present-day El Paso, Texas. At the Yaqui River, they spotted an Indian wearing a curious object on his belt. They looked closely and discovered it was a Spanish-made horseshoe nail. Castillo took the object from the Indian, and the men asked the Indian how he got it. The Spaniards were told that other men had come on horses with lances and swords to that river and had killed two Indians with lance thrusts. The Indians said that these men then went to sea, and the last they saw of them, they were on top of the waves and going towards the sunset.

Cabeza de Vaca and his men knew they were near Spanish civilization. They hurried on, always finding evidence along the trail that other Spaniards had been there. They also found the country along the route deserted: The natives had abandoned their villages and fled to the moun-

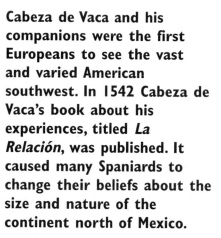

Cabeza de Vaca and his companions were the first Europeans to see the vast and varied American southwest. In 1542 Cabeza de Vaca's book about his experiences, titled *La Relación*, was published. It caused many Spaniards to change their beliefs about the size and nature of the continent north of Mexico.

tains. The Indians they encountered told the four travelers how the Spaniards had come, burned their villages, and taken away all the women and children and half the men, and that the rest were fugitives. The four wondered if the natives would take revenge upon them. Instead, they took

Cabeza de Vaca and his companions to an encampment on the crest of a mountain and fed them.

In September 1534, Cabeza de Vaca and some of his men broke away from a site which is now the modern city of San Antonio. They wintered with a tribe in South Texas called the Avavares, another hunting and gathering group. The Avavares fed the four *venison*, which they had never eaten before. While looking for food, Cabeza de Vaca almost died. He lost his way and became very cold. He found a burning tree, probably ignited by lightning, which he stoked for warmth. Over the next few days, he carried firebrands and dry sticks with him to stay warm. Cabeza de Vaca and his group of men stayed with the Avavares for eight months.

After leaving the Avavares, Cabeza de Vaca's group crossed the Rio Grande into Mexico. Shortly after departing Texas, they saw the first mountains they had encountered on the North American continent. Instead of continuing down the coast, they chose to turn inland. While crossing northern Mexico, Cabeza de Vaca performed the first surgery to be done by a

Cabeza de Vaca grew tired of his role as healer and medicine man, saying that it was exhausting to have to breathe on and make signs of the cross over every morsel the Native Americans ate or drank.

European in the American southwest. An Indian had been wounded by an arrow that entered the right side of his back and lodged over the heart. Using a knife, Cabeza de Vaca opened the chest, took out the arrowhead, and closed the cut with two stitches. He stopped the bleeding using hair scraped from the skin of an animal.

In July 1536, near Culiacan in present-day Sinaloa, they met a group of fellow Spaniards who were on a slave-taking expedition. As Cabeza de Vaca remembered, his country-men were "dumbfounded at the sight of me, strangely dressed and in the company of Indians. They stood staring for a long time."

The Spanish commander, Diego de Alcaraz, was delight-ed to see the 600 Pima Indians with Cabeza de Vaca. He hadn't been able to catch Indians in a long time and want-ed one of Cabeza de Vaca's guides. Cabeza de Vaca refused, however. If Indians were to be converted, he said, "they must be won by kindness, the only certain way." Cabeza de Vaca told the Indian followers to return home and replant their crops, but they didn't want to leave their healer among these Spaniards. Cabeza de Vaca finally convinced the Pimas to go home, but the slavers waited until Cabeza de Vaca and his men were on their way, then seized many of the Indians for slaves.

For two days, Cabeza de Vaca and his companions were

The Spanish Exploration of the Southwest

Antonio de Mendoza was the first viceroy, or colonial governor, of New Spain. His laws provided a foundation for three centuries of Spanish rule in Mexico and the American southwest.

led through timber, away from the trail and without water. They were taken in by Melchior Díaz, the authority at Culiacan. Cabeza de Vaca told Díaz about what Alcaraz was doing. Díaz sent messengers to find the Indians who had been taken captive. The messengers returned with three chiefs and 15 other men, who reported that the people who dwelt along the river had again all fled to the mountains to escape the slave hunters. Díaz talked for a long time with the Indians. He assured them of his good will and promised them that if they would reoccupy their villages, build churches, and accept missionaries, they would be protected and treated as brothers. About a week later, Alcaraz reported that the Indians were obeying instructions, reoccupying their villages, building churches, and tilling their fields.

When Cabeza de Vaca's party arrived in Mexico City, they were welcomed as heroes by the viceroy of New Spain, Antonio de Mendoza. Although Cabeza de Vaca had only experienced hardship on his trip, he told tales of fabulous riches, perhaps to impress people. He said the Seven Cities were beyond the region where he had traveled. Indian tribal leaders had told him that far to the north were wealthy nations whose citizens lived in huge houses. Emeralds, turquoises, and other rare gems lay on the ground there, he said the Indians had told him.

Cabeza de Vaca also told of the gifts presented to him by the Pima people. "To me, they gave five emeralds made into arrowheads, which they used at singing and dancing. . . . I asked them where they got these; and they said the stones were brought from some lofty mountains that stand toward the north, where there were populous towns of large houses." Unfortunately, Cabeza de Vaca had lost these valuable gems during his travels, so it was never established whether the green arrowheads were genuine emeralds or, in fact, *malachite*.

In 1539, a Spanish expedition led by a priest named Marcos de Niza reported a rich kingdom in the southwest. According to reports from Indian guides, the cities of this land were filled with stone houses three and four stories high, decorated with turquoise, gold, and silver. The cities of Cibola were actually Zuni Indian pueblos, like this one in New Mexico.

On the Heels of Cabeza de Vaca

EAGER TO FIND new wealth for Spain, the viceroy sent out a new expedition. This one was headed by a Spanish priest named Fray Marcos de Niza. Estéban, the black slave who had survived with Cabeza de Vaca, would be his guide. Estéban wore a bright-colored robe and a hat adorned with rare feathers. At his side was his rattle. Estéban and Marcos de Niza worked out a code. Estéban would scout the region, leading a small troop of Native Americans miles ahead of Fray Marcos and the rest of the group. When Estéban spotted an Indian community, he was to send back a runner bearing a wooden cross. The larger the cross, the larger the settlement.

As the men marched north and approached the border of the present-day state of New Mexico, Fray Marcos saw a messenger approaching. The runner was staggering under the weight of a huge cross. The runner told Marcos that Estéban had learned of a marvelous country. The slave had not seen it, but the Indians they had met swore it was there. It was called Cibola.

In late 1539, the priest received news from messengers covered with wounds. They said Estéban and his Indians had been attacked when they approached a Zuni Indian city. Estéban had been killed.

According to stories told by the Zuni Indians of the region, Zuni families in the city of Háwikuh had been planning their planting ritual when they saw 300 Indians coming. They were escorting a tall, dark-skinned man who was dressed in **pelts** and wearing bits of turquoise. He was walking two greyhounds on a leash. His escorts said he was a healer, but the people of Háwikuh tried to block his entry by pouring a line of sacred cornmeal across the path. The stranger stepped over it, declaring himself a Child of the Sun. He wanted turquoise and women and warned that more of the Sun's children were on their way. As a token of his power, he showed them a decorated gourd rattle.

The chief of the pueblo recognized the rattle as having been made by a people far to the south whom he disliked.

Fray Marcos de Niza

Fray Marcos de Niza was born in Nice, France in 1495. After becoming a Franciscan friar, he traveled to the New World in 1531. He served as a Spanish missionary in Peru, Guatemala, and Mexico before being chosen to explore the country to the north of New Spain.

In 1538, Viceroy Antonio de Mendoza entrusted him with the task of investigating rumors of wealthy cities beyond the northern frontiers of New Spain—rumors fueled by the recent return of Alvar Núñez Cabeza de Vaca. Fray Marcos left Culiacan in March 1539. He traveled to a settlement called Vacapa, which is close to the present-day Mexican states of Sinaloa and Sonora. His guide Estéban was sent ahead, and sent back messages about the rich kingdom called Cibola. From a distance, Marcos himself saw one of the Zuni villages, which he described as being equal in size to the capital of New Spain, Mexico City.

His report to Antonio de Mendoza, titled *Descubrimiento de las siete cuidades* (Description of the seven cities), led Francisco Vásquez de Coronado to lead his own expedition the next year. Fray Marcos joined him on this journey, which proved to be a great disappointment.

Fray Marcos was later given a high position in the Franciscan order in New Spain. He died on March 25, 1558, after suffering from poor health for a decade.

He believed the stranger to be either a spy, a madman, or a witch, and ordered Estéban killed. Afterwards, the pueblo people wondered if they had done the right thing. They were now worried about the Children of the Sun.

When Fray Marcos found out Estéban had been killed, he wanted to hurry back to Mexico. Before he fled, though, he wanted to see a glimpse of Háwikuh. He looked down from a hill in present-day New Mexico and saw what he believed to be a vast city. When he returned home, Fray Marcos told the authorities in Mexico what he had seen.

In the meantime, Cabeza de Vaca had returned to Spain. He hoped to convince the king to make him **adelantado**, or ruler, of Florida. However, by the time he got home the king had already given this position to Hernando de Soto. De Soto offered Cabeza de Vaca the job as second in command of the expedition, but Cabeza de Vaca turned him down.

The Zunis did not like the _requirimento_, a Spanish demand that the Native Americans acknowledge the Catholic Church as leader of the whole world, the Pope as high priest, and in his name, the King and Queen of Spain as rulers. The _requirimento_ warned the Zuni that if they failed to obey orders, "with the help of God we shall forcefully make war against you, take you and your wives and children, and shall make slaves of them."

The Last Years of Cabeza de Vaca

On March 8, 1540, Cabeza de Vaca was named governor of what is now Paraguay, in South America. He established a Spanish outpost there at the site of the present-day city of Asunción, surviving by trading with the villages of the Guarani tribe. In January 1542, he and his men followed the Parana River to where it meets the Paraguay River. Cabeza de Vaca then took several of his men and traveled by land back to Asunción. They arrived on March 11, 1542, to the great joy of the settlers, who thought they had been abandoned.

Cabeza de Vaca believed it would be possible to open a route along the Paraguay River to the rich gold mines and cities in Peru. He set out with a new expedition in September 1543. They stoped at a place he called Puerto de los Reyes, or Port of the Kings. Cabeza de Vaca was soon forced to return by his followers, who did not want to risk the jungle.

Two weeks after he returned to Asunción, Cabeza de Vaca was thrown out of office by a rebel governor, who imprisoned him and then sent him to Spain in 1545. He was found guilty of corruption, perhaps because of his good conduct toward the Indians, and he was banished to Africa for eight years. His wife spent all her fortune on his behalf, and finally the king revoked the sentence. The 1552 pardon allowed him to become a judge in Seville, Spain, a position that he occupied until his death in 1556 or 1557.

Hernando de Soto

Hernando de Soto had been born around 1499 in the Estremadura province of Spain. As a young man, he sailed to Central America with Pedro Arias de Avila, who had been named ade-

lantado of the region. De Soto became a soldier, fighting the natives of Central America.

When Francisco Pizarro set out to find the Inca empire in Peru, de Soto accompanied him. With the conquest of the Incas, de Soto became one of the richest men in Spain.

In 1537 the king of Spain named de Soto adelantado of Cuba and Florida. De Soto prepared carefully for his expedition to Florida. He even invited Cabeza de Vaca to join him as second in command, but the explorer declined.

De Soto landed in Florida in May 1539 with about 700 men. In their search for gold, the Spaniards wandered through Florida, then north as far as the present-day states of North Carolina and Tennessee. The party then turned west. By 1542, de Soto had found the Mississippi River and the party had roamed into present-day Texas. De Soto died in May of that year, and the survivors of his expedition returned to New Spain in September 1543.

In 1542, Cabeza de Vaca's book about his experiences in the New World was published. In *La Relación*, Cabeza de Vaca wrote about the region's potential for farming, raising sheep and cattle, and mining—especially for gold, silver, emeralds, and turquoises. He also believed that a fabulous *aboriginal* nation existed in the north, not too far beyond the perimeter of his journeys, and that another was on the Pacific, which was much nearer the northern pueblos. This information convinced other men to explore.

But even before the book was published, the tales Cabeza de Vaca had told about the legendary Seven Cities of Cibola encouraged other expeditions to America. One of the most highly regarded explorers was a young man named Francisco Vásquez de Coronado.

In the summer of 1540, Francisco Vásquez de Coronado split up his force, sending small scouting parties in different directions looking for the Seven Cities of Cibola. A group commanded by Garcia López de Cárdenas became the first Europeans to see the Grand Canyon—one of many wonders the Spaniards of Coronado's expedition would find in the southwest.

Rumors of Treasure

ON FEBRUARY 23, 1540, a force of Spanish soldiers set out from Compostela in New Spain. The small army included 225 horsemen, 62 infantrymen, and some 1,300 male and female servants and retainers. Many of these slaves were Native Americans from the Tlaxcalan tribe or Africans. The Spanish party also brought 1,000 horses and mules and a large number of sheep, goats, and cattle. Their leader wore **gilded** armor and a steel helmet adorned with feathers. His name was Francisco Coronado.

Coronado was a trusted friend of the viceroy of New Spain, Antonio de Mendoza. The small army had been sent north by Mendoza to find the fabled Seven Cities of Gold.

Antonio de Mendoza

Antonio de Mendoza was born in Granada, Spain in 1490. He was related to the king and came from a leading Spanish family. He served as the Spanish ambassador to Rome and was commissioned as viceroy of New Spain (Mexico) in 1530.

Mendoza was interested in the Seven Cities of Gold, rumored to exist to the north of New Spain. The wealth there was supposed to far exceed even that of the Aztecs and the Incas. A friar named Marcos de Niza told others that he had traveled to the kingdom, where he saw a gleaming city that local Indians had described as the smallest of the seven. This inspired the expedition of Francisco Coronado.

As viceroy of New Spain, Mendoza encouraged education. He sensed the Indians' intellectual potential during those first days when he arrived in Mexico and an Indian boy had greeted him in classical Latin. Mendoza helped create two institutions. One was the Colegio de Santa Cruz de Tlateloco, which he founded in 1536 along with Bishop Juan de Zumarraga. Students there were the sons of Indian nobles. They received instruction in such subjects as Latin and philosophy. The other school was the Royal and Pontifical University of Mexico, also co-founded with Bishop Zumarraga. This institution trained young Creoles for the clergy.

Mendoza died in 1552.

Many of the Indians were wearing the cotton body protectors favored by their people in central Mexico. The rest of the army was wearing armor and carried fine Toledo swords, iron-headed lances, bows, and shields. There were a few *arquebuses* and powerful crossbows, but those weapons were expensive.

Coronado and his men proceeded up the west coast of Mexico to Culiacan, a northern outpost of New Galicia. From there, the expedition entered what is now the United States in April 1540 along the San Pedro River at the southern end of the Huachuca Mountains.

Coronado had been told that the land was level and that food and water supplies would be abundant. However, the opposite was true. There were many marches where the trails were difficult and the trails nearly impassable, with little food for the men and animals. At times, the route wore out the sheep and goats, and they had to be left behind. Horses lost their footing and slipped from the cliffs.

The adventurers spent close to four months straggling through 800 miles of mountains, jungle, and flooded streams to the official starting point at Culiacan, located a short distance inland from Mexico's west coast, opposite the lower end of Baja California.

Coronado's assistant Melchior Díaz, stationed at the provincial capital, had recently led a squad of soldiers north from Culiacan to learn more about the expedition's route to Cibola. Fray Marcos's earlier account had said that a good road followed the coast, so that ships could be used to supply the land party. Because of this, Antonio de Mendoza had equipped three small vessels. These would be used to take supplies up the California coast, where the ships would meet Coronado's troops.

Unfortunately, Díaz had bad news when he met Coronado at Culiacan. Contrary to Marcos's report, the road was not very good and it veered to the east, away from the coast. By the time Coronado reached Háwikuh, he would be far away from the supply ships.

Coronado decided to leave most of his army at Culiacan, under the command of Tristan de Arellano. He and Díaz moved ahead in April 1840 with a party of 80 horsemen, a few foot soldiers, four *friars*, hundreds of Indians, and some of their livestock.

It took 11 weeks for Coronado and his men to travel the 1,000 miles north to Cibola. In July 1540, the Spanish cavalry came upon the Zuni pueblo of Háwikuh in the western part of present-day New Mexico. Coronado and his party had arrived during the high point of Zuni summer ceremonies, and outsiders were not welcome.

The Zuni saw Coronado and his companions coming with the sun slanting off their helmets and believed they

Francisco Coronado

Francisco Vásquez de Coronado was born to a noble family in Salamanca, Spain, in 1510. As a young man at court, he became friendly with Antonio de Mendoza. When Mendoza was appointed viceroy of New Spain (Mexico) in 1535, Coronado accompanied him to America as his assistant.

Within three years of his arrival in Mexico City, Mendoza had ordered Coronado to put down a rebellion among Indians and black slaves who had taken over a silver mine. Coronado handled this job so well that Mendoza named him governor of New Galicia in 1538. Coronado also married the wealthy Beatriz Estrada, daughter of New Spain's treasurer, which gained him an enormous estate. Beatriz was beautiful as well as wealthy. During her lifetime she was known for her *piety* and good works and was nicknamed "the saint."

Coronado was 29 when he led an expedition to find the Seven Cities of Cibola. He paid for a large portion of the expedition himself, borrowing 50,000 ducats (about a million dollars in today's money) from his wealthy wife. Viceroy Mendoza also invested 60,000 ducats of his own money in his friend's expedition. He had no reason to believe it was a risky investment.

might be the Children of the Sun that Estéban had warned them of. The Zuni had never seen horses before and were

The Hopi knew the white man was coming. They knew that Taiowa, the creator, had made four races of men: black, red, yellow, and white. Their legend had it that long ago the races had separated, but that one day, Pahana—the lost white brother from across the water—would return. The Hopi knew what to do if Pahana came. The Hopi chief would hold out his hand palm up. Pahana would clasp his hand in a special way of universal brotherhood. When Coronado sent Pedro de Tovar to the Hopi, their wise man put out his hand in the special way. Tovar dropped a little present in it. Thus, the Hopi knew this was not Pahana.

astounded. Coronado told them through an interpreter that he had come on a sacred mission. He warned that they must submit to the Spanish crown and Christianity. The Zuni refused to let them enter the pueblo. Some Zuni might have heard from trading partners to the south about Spanish slavers, while others may have believed that the Spaniards had come to avenge the death of Estéban.

The Zuni began firing arrows at the Spaniards, at one point nearly killing Coronado himself. "They grew so bold that they came up almost to the heels of our horses to shoot their arrows. On this account, I saw that it was no longer time to hesitate, and as the priests approved the action, I charged them," Coronado reported. But

Coronado's shiny gold armor made him a tempting target, and he was hit by a large stone hurled from a rooftop.

The Spaniards had to climb ladders to get at the Indians, who were fighting from the flat roofs of the pueblo buildings. The men were tired and could hardly work their crossbows and arquebuses. However, hunger drove them onward. The Indians' wooden weapons were no match for the Spaniards' steel swords and horses, and soon the Zuni were forced to flee.

The victors examined their prize: a barren plaza, mud houses, skimpy furnishings that would bring scarcely a peso in Mexico City. They cursed Fray Marcos. However, they did find one valuable item in the city: food. One soldier recounted that they found "something we prized much more than gold or silver; namely plentiful maize and beans and turkeys larger than those in New Spain, and salt better and whiter than I have ever seen in my whole life."

Coronado called a meeting of the chief men of the Zuni pueblos and sought to learn from them about the surrounding countryside. The Indians said the regional cities were big and rich, especially those occupied by the Hopi to the northwest. To top that, a pair of *emissaries* arrived from a Towa village located beside the Pecos River 200 miles to the east. The two had heard of the strangers' arrival and had hurried west to discover what had been going on. From

These stone walls mark the ruins of Háwikuh, once a thriving Zuni town in the southwest. Though Coronado and his men captured the town, they found no gold or other riches.

them, Coronado learned that there were many pueblos. Surely some of them were rich.

Coronado dispatched one party northwest to the Hopi villages, which he called the Kingdom of Tusayan. The Hopi lived on four high mesas, or *plateaus*, from which they descended to cultivate their fields and to obtain water. A scuffle broke out between the Hopi and the soldiers. Eventually, the Indians surrendered. The Hopi later told them about a great river to the west.

When Coronado was staying at Háwikuh, Indians came from the east. They lived in a pueblo called Cicuye, near what is now Santa Fe, New Mexico. Cicuye was a large pueblo on the eastern bank of a creek between nearby mountains and had about 50 houses. The Indians from Cicuye brought the Spaniards a present of tanned hides and shields and headpieces. These were gladly received, and Coronado gave them some glass dishes and a number of pearls and little bells, which they prized highly because these were things they had never seen. One chief the Spanish nicknamed Bigotes, or Whiskers, for his long mustache. Coronado sent Hernando de Alvarado and 20 men east with Bigotes to explore. Alvarado found villages around the Rio Grande and sent a message to Coronado saying Tiguex (present-day Bernalillo near Albuquerque) would be a good place to spend the winter.

Coronado moved the entire army to Tiguex, where he sheltered his men by forcing the Indians out of their pueblos. The Spaniards also took whatever food and clothing they needed from the Native Americans. There were several fierce attacks by the Tiguex Indians, but the Spaniards put down these "revolts." However, bad feelings would remain between the natives and Spaniards.

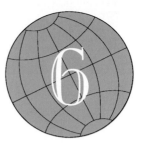

Coronado and his men set up a wooden cross by the banks of a river in this magazine illustration. Hoping that his expedition would not end in failure, Coronado traveled far to the northeast seeking the rich city of Quivira. However, he was forced to return to New Spain empty-handed.

The Return of Coronado's Expedition

IN THE SPRING of 1541, the force moved into the Palo Duro Canyon in present-day Texas, where Coronado left most of his men, and proceeded north with 30 horsemen to another supposedly fabulously wealthy country, Quivira. Coronado had met an Indian, whom he called "the Turk," who told him about Quivira. The Turk offered to lead the men of Coronado to this place.

Coronado crossed the Texas panhandle and marched further north. He encountered *nomadic* hunters who used troops of dogs to drag their belongings. They also saw the American bison, or buffalo, and described it for the first time. Coronado led his comrades through an ocean of grass so vast and featureless they had to navigate using a sea compass onto the great plain of what is now Kansas. They also had to make piles of bones and cow dung so that the rear guard could follow the army.

However, Quivira had no treasures. The Wichita village (near present-day Lindsborg, Kansas) was merely huts surrounded by beans and cornfields. The Turk was lying, or at least Coronado thought he was. The Indians here were dark-skinned, tattooed, and nearly naked. The Quivira Indians (later known as the Wichita) were no rich people at all; the village consisted mostly of scattered round lodges roofed with grass and emitting smoke from holes in the roofs. Not even small amounts of gold could be found among them. There were no bells tinkling from trees, no fishes big as horses, and no boats with golden prows. Quivira did, however, have rich black soil, beautiful rivulets, and springs and rivers. Coronado found nuts and plums and sweet grapes and mulberries to eat. Cows had humped backs, and the Indians of the region ate their buffalo meat raw. There, Coronado raised a great stone cross and chiseled a message on it that said Francisco Vásquez de

Coronado's search for Quivira took him as far to the northeast as central Kansas. Pieces of Spanish armor have been found at several places in the state.

The Turk, an Indian of the Plains who accompanied Coronado's expedition, points the Spaniards in the direction of Quivira in this book illustration. The Native American got his name because the headpiece he wore reminded the Spaniards of the turbans worn by Muslims from Turkey.

Coronado, general of the army, had arrived. The Spanish then marched away in August 1541. Coronado returned to Tiguex, where his main force had remained. Here, he spent another winter.

After realizing that the Seven Cities of Cibola were only the Zuni, Hopi, and Pueblo Indian villages of present-day Arizona and New Mexico, the expedition started homeward. The villages were not the "land of gold and silver where the lord of the realm took his siesta under a tree covered with a myriad of tiny gold bells, which tinkled in the breeze, lulling him to sleep," as the Turk had told him. The

This painting is from a kiva at Kuaua pueblo, which has been preserved at Coronado State Park, New Mexico. A kiva was an underground chamber used in the pueblo for ceremonies.

Turk was later strangled by Coronado's men for lying. Coronado and his companions returned to Mexico on the Rio Grande. While there, Coronado suffered a fall from his horse, which injured his head seriously. It left him with little energy. He led only about 100 men into Mexico City in 1542, while the remainder straggled in over the following months. He reported his disappointing findings to Mendoza, who turned on his old protégé and branded the expedition an abject failure.

An official inquiry forced Coronado to face a trial for his conduct, but he was found not guilty. Coronado remained in his position as governor of New Galicia until he was *indicted* again. In 1544, he was found guilty of corruption, negligence, and **atrocities** against the Native Americans under his authority. Coronado returned to Mexico City, where he worked in a modest position in the municipal government. He died on September 22 at the age of 44. Coronado was buried in Mexico City at Santa Domingo Church.

Coronado's travels have had a great impact on the settlement and history of the American West. For example, he brought horses to the southwest. These animals would quickly change the lifestyles of the Plains Indians. Though Coronado died in disgrace, his excursions have proven to be one of the more important feats of the Spanish conquest in America. They opened up a vast new world to eventual settlement by Europeans—a tribute to the genius of Antonio de Mendoza.

Chronology

1480 Alvar Núñez Cabeza de Vaca is born.

1510 Francisco Vásquez de Coronado is born in Salmanca, Spain.

1513 Juan Ponce de León claims Florida for Spain.

1521 Hernán Cortés conquers the Aztec empire in Mexico and establishes New Spain.

1526 The Spanish conquistador Pánfilo de Narváez is given permission to explore the region known as La Florida; Cabeza de Vaca is named treasurer of the expedition.

1528 The Narváez expedition lands in Florida in April; after exploring Florida, the men build boats and attempt to follow the coast south to New Spain. Narváez is drowned in October, and Cabeza de Vaca is shipwrecked with 80 other Spaniards on Galveston Island.

1529 In April 13 Spanish survivors of the Narváez expedition set out for Mexico, leaving Cabeza de Vaca and another man behind. Cabeza spends the next four years with Native Americans in this region, becoming a trader.

1532 Cabeza de Vaca is reunited with Alonso de Castillo, Andrés Dorantes, and Estéban.

1536 Cabeza de Vaca and his three companions arrive in New Spain, where he tells the viceroy, Antonio de Mendoza, about the lands of the American southwest.

Chronology

1539 A Franciscan friar named Marcos de Niza is sent with Estéban to gather information about the Seven Cities of Cibola. Estéban is reported to have been killed by the Zuni Indians, but Marcos returns with news of a large city, Háwikuh.

1540 Francisco Vásquez de Coronado sets out from Compostela, reaching Háwikuh in July. The Spaniards capture the town, but Coronado is wounded. He sends small groups of soldiers in different directions, and although they do not find gold or rich cities, they do return with information about the Grand Canyon, the Colorado River, and Hopi villages in present-day Arizona. The Spaniards spend the winter at Tiguex.

1541 Coronado and his men search for the city of Quivira, traveling into present-day Kansas. Unsuccessful in their quest for gold, the army returns to Tiguex for another winter.

1542 Coronado returns to Mexico City, where he gives Mendoza the disappointing news. He is later tried for mismanaging the expedition, but found not guilty.

Glossary

aboriginal—the original natives of a region.

adelantado—a Spanish governor or ruler of a region.

arquebus—a matchlock gun invented in the 15th century that was portable but heavy and was usually fired from a support.

atrocity—a shockingly cruel act, especially an act of extreme violence.

conquistador—a leader in the Spanish conquest of America in the 16th century.

desert—to run away from an armed force or military post without permission and intending never to go back.

emissary—one who serves as the representative of another.

friar—a member of a religious order.

gilded—covered with a thin layer of gold or another shiny substance.

gourd—the inedible fruit of certain plants which have hard rinds and are often used as ornaments or for vessels and utensils.

indict—to formally accuse somebody of wrongdoing.

interpreter—somebody who translates orally what is said in one language into another language, so that speakers of different languages can communicate.

Glossary

malachite—a mineral that is a green basic carbonate of copper used as an ore and for making ornamental objects.

nomadic—roaming about from place to place aimlessly, frequently, or without a fixed pattern of movement.

ochre—an iron ore used as a coloring; it is earthy, usually red or yellow, and often impure.

pelt—the skin of an animal, often with its hair, wool, or fur still attached, which can be worn as clothing.

piety—devoutness, especially to one's religion.

plateau—a large land area having a relatively level surface and raised sharply above nearby land on at least one side.

provisions—a stock of needed materials and supplies, especially food.

spoils—loot taken from an enemy in war.

venison—the edible flesh of deer.

Further Reading

Howard, David A. *Conquistador in Chains: Cabeza de Vaca and the Indians of North America.* Tuscaloosa: University of Alabama Press, 1997.

Marcovitz, Hal. *Francisco Coronado and the Exploration of the American Southwest.* Philadelphia: Chelsea House, 2000.

Thompson, Bill, and Dorcas Thompson. *The Spanish Exploration of Florida.* Philadelphia: Mason Crest, 2003.

Ward, Geoffrey C. *The West.* West Book Project, 1996.

Wilson, James. *The Earth Shall Weep: A History of Native America.* New York: Grove Press, 1998.

Internet Resources

Francisco Vásquez de Coronado

http://www.win.tue.nl/~engels/discovery/coronado.html

http://www.pbs.org/weta/thewest/people/a_c/coronado.htm

http://www.lsjunction.com/people/coronado.htm

http://www.desertusa.com/mag98/sep/papr/coronado.html

Alvar Núñez Cabeza de Vaca

http://www.english.swt.edu/CSS/Vacaindex.HTML

http://www.floridahistory.com/cabeza.html

http://www.pbs.org/weta/thewest/people/a_c/cabezadevaca.htm

http://www.mediasrv.swt.edu/cabaza/Cabeza_Home.html

Antonio de Mendoza

http://www.rice.edu/armadillo/Projects/mendoza.html

Index

Photo Credits

page

6:	Giraudon/Art Resource, NY	28–29:	Corbis Images
8:	Courtesy The Mariners' Museum, Newport News, VA	32:	Scala/Art Resource, NY
		34:	MIT Collection/Corbis
		40:	North Wind Picture Archives
9:	Library of Congress	42:	Hulton/Archive
12:	Giraudon/Art Resource, NY	50:	Jan Butchofsky-Houser/ Corbis
16–17:	Corbis		
18:	Art Resource, NY	52:	Bettmann/Corbis
20:	North Wind Picture Archives	55:	Corbis
25:	Hulton/Archive	56:	Corbis

Front cover: Hulton/Archive
Back cover: Hulton/Archive; Giraudon/Art Resource, NY; Bettmann/Corbis

About the Author

Lenore Wilson teaches creative writing at Napa Valley College. She lives on the family cattle ranch. Her work has been featured in many national and international magazines. Her creative non-fiction recently won a first-prize fellowship in the Writers at Work Conference sponsored by *Quarterly West*. Her pride and joy are her three sons.